PLANET UNDER SIEGE:
CLIMATE CHANGE

Don Nardo

ReferencePoint Press®

San Diego, CA

© 2020 ReferencePoint Press, Inc.
Printed in the United States

For more information, contact:
ReferencePoint Press, Inc.
PO Box 27779
San Diego, CA 92198
www.ReferencePointPress.com

LIBRARY OF CONGRESS CATALOGING-IN-PUBLICATION DATA

Name: Nardo, Don, 1947– author.
Title: Planet Under Siege: Climate Change/Don Nardo.
Other titles: Climate change
Description: San Diego: ReferencePoint Press, 2019. | Includes
    bibliographical references and index. | Audience: Grades 10-12.
Identifiers: LCCN 2019023443 (print) | LCCN 2019023444 (ebook) | ISBN
    9781682827574 (library binding) | ISBN 9781682827581 (ebook)
Subjects: LCSH: Climatic changes—Juvenile literature. | Climatic
    extremes—Environmental aspects—Juvenile literature.
Classification: LCC QC903.15 .N3725 2019 (print) | LCC QC903.15 (ebook) |
    DDC 363.738/74—dc23
LC record available at https://lccn.loc.gov/2019023443
LC ebook record available at https://lccn.loc.gov/2019023444

CONTENTS

Climate Change Is Already Happening

The US Department of Defense (DOD) oversees the deadliest military machine in the world, and indeed in human history. The United States spends more on its armed forces and is more powerful than the next seven strongest countries combined. Yet, US military leaders point out, all that vast firepower is useless against an enemy that presently threatens not only the United States but *all* nations. That enemy is climate change.

In January 2019 the DOD announced its newest report on the increasing global challenge of climate change. Dozens of US military bases are presently threatened by conditions driven by climate change, the report stated. Among them are rising sea levels, huge wildfires, and severe droughts. The report also explained how US military operations are already being disrupted in various ways by climate-related effects. The overall thrust of the report was that climate change is already a very real threat to national security—and this danger will only increase in the near future.

The DOD's findings echoed those of most of the world's climate scientists as well as dozens of major scientific organizations and university research facilities that study climate change. The US Global Change Research Program (USGCRP), for example, a group tasked by Congress to study the forces shaping the global environment, said in its 2018 report,

Earth's climate is now changing faster than at any point in the history of modern civilization, primarily as a result of human activities. Global climate change has already resulted in a wide range of impacts across every region of the country and many sectors of the economy that are expected to grow in the coming decades [including] human health, agriculture and food security, water supply, transportation, energy, ecosystems, and others.[1]

In stark contrast to these dire warnings by experts, President Donald Trump continued, as he had in the past, to deride climate change—often also called *global warming*—as a hoax. Only a few days after the DOD released its 2019 report, Trump pointed out that a major winter storm was at that moment wreaking havoc in the Midwest. He declared in a tweet, "Large parts of the Country are suffering from tremendous amounts of snow and near record setting cold. Amazing how big this [cold weather] system is. Wouldn't be bad to have a little of that good old fashioned Global Warming right now!"[2]

"Wouldn't be bad to have a little of that good old fashioned Global Warming right now!"[2]

—President Donald Trump

Climate vs. Weather

Both DOD officials and climate scientists were disappointed that the president once more repeated a common mistake made by many nonscientists. Namely, he confused *climate* and *weather*. Contrary to what many people assume, they are not the same thing. Weather is a local phenomenon. It is made up of changing temperatures and increases and decreases in rain and other precipitation in a given region at a given point in time. The weather in that area will be different the following day or following week, and cities and regions around the world will all exhibit very different weather outlooks at any given time.

In contrast, global climate is a much larger, more consistent phenomenon that exists worldwide and overrides local weather differences. One way to understand global climate is to think of

Due to climate change, hurricanes are growing steadily stronger. This photo, taken in 2018, shows the damage from Hurricane Michael in Mexico Beach, Florida.

it as the overall temperature of the planet's atmosphere. Local temperatures near ground level will differ widely from day to day. Some regions will be very hot while more distant regions are very cold. But the atmosphere as a whole maintains an average temperature. That helps to determine the temperatures of the oceans, which in turn affect the weather patterns on the continents.

Normally, the global climate remains more or less stable for long periods. It can and does change sometimes; in fact, Earth has undergone several big and small climate changes in past ages. But usually these variations happened slowly, over the course of many centuries or millennia. Also, the changes were caused by natural forces, such as continent-building forces, long-term increases or decreases in incoming solar radiation, and major volcanic activity.

A Greenhouse on a Much Bigger Scale

The problem with the present case of climate change is that it is taking place extremely fast from a geologic point of view—in the space of only a few centuries or even a few decades. Moreover, the main cause is not natural. Instead, human activity—especially heavy industrialization during the past couple centuries—has caused the planetary atmosphere to grow warmer.

A number of atmospheric and geologic processes work together to make this happen. By far, however, the most prevalent one is the so-called greenhouse effect. Scientists coined that term to explain why a greenhouse stays warm inside, even in the winter. The same effect happens in the atmosphere, they explain, only on a much bigger scale. According to the US space agency, NASA, one of the organizations that has closely examined climate change,

> In the daytime, sunlight shines into the greenhouse and warms the plants and air inside. At nighttime, it's colder outside, but the greenhouse stays pretty warm inside. That's because the glass walls of the greenhouse trap the sun's heat. The greenhouse effect works much the same way on earth. Gases in the atmosphere, such as carbon dioxide, trap heat just like the glass roof of a greenhouse. These heat-trapping gases are called greenhouse gases.[3]

Although there are many greenhouse gases, the primary ones are carbon dioxide and methane. For more than two centuries, factories, cars, trucks, and other human-made sources have pumped huge amounts of carbon dioxide into the atmosphere. At the same time, billions of cattle and other farm animals have released methane in their flatulence. These substances have slowly but steadily increased the atmosphere's mean temperature. According to the National Oceanic and Atmospheric Association (NOAA), "The average global temperature during 2018 was 1.42 degrees F above the 20th-century average. This marks the 42nd consecutive year (since 1977) with an above-average global temperature. Nine of the 10 warmest years have occurred since 2005, with the last five years comprising the five hottest."[4]

Serious Large-Scale Consequences

A rise of less than two degrees might not sound like much. And, in the context of the daily weather report, it really does not mean much of anything (other than that it will be a couple degrees warmer that day). When it comes to global climate, however, even a two-degree difference (built up over just a few decades) has serious large-scale consequences. Those consequences are already being felt around the world.

First, as the atmosphere warms up, it holds far more moisture than before. That moisture means more rain and hot weather in some regions and more snow and cold weather in other regions. In other words, the other term for climate change—*global warming*—is a misnomer. Climate change will not make all places hotter, as that term suggests. It will instead cause massive weather extremes, with bitterly cold winters in some areas and drought in others. These increases in atmospheric precipitation are causing so-called hundred-year floods almost every year in some parts of the United States.

Meanwhile, the negative effects of climate change are growing more and more apparent over time. Glaciers and polar ice caps are melting and shrinking, causing sea levels to rise. Miami, Florida, is only one of many cities worldwide that are already seeing loss of coastal land to the oceans. Those seas are growing warmer as well, which is already causing hurricanes to markedly increase in intensity. Also, forest fires intensified by climate change–driven droughts have gotten so big that they are visible from space. In addition, hundreds of animal species are on the brink of extinction due to climate change's effects, a threat to nature's delicate balance of biodiversity.

Denial Is No Longer an Option

The reaction of most countries to the impending crisis has been a realization that humanity must do whatever is necessary to halt climate change, or at least significantly slow its progress. To

The Greta Thunberg Effect

Few individuals have sounded the alarm about ongoing climate change more loudly and sharply than a Swedish teenager named Greta Thunberg. In August 2018, at the age of fifteen, she began protesting outside the Swedish parliament building in Stockholm. Her demands for people worldwide to take the issue of climate change more seriously swiftly attracted the attention of media worldwide.

Thereafter she spearheaded a global youth movement. In November 2018 its members staged the first of their so-called school strikes to protest government inaction on climate change. Thousands of young climate change activists and other concerned citizens protested in dozens of cities around the globe. Thunberg and her followers helped to organize a much bigger demonstration on March 15, 2019, in which an estimated 1.4 million students from 112 countries took part. A similar international event occurred on May 24, 2019, this time featuring young people from 125 nations.

Thunberg has received numerous awards and honors for her climate change activities. In March 2019, members of Norway's parliament nominated her for a Nobel Peace Prize, and she appeared on the cover of *Time* magazine the following May. Her ability to inspire people, both young and old, to become activists for confronting the dangers of climate change has come to be known as "the Greta Thunberg effect."

that end, in 2015 more than 190 nations adopted a pact called the Paris Agreement. The signers, including the United States, pledged to steadily cut back on releases of greenhouse gases over time.

In 2017, however, a new US president, Donald Trump, pulled the country out of the Paris Agreement. In so doing, he tapped into a strongly ingrained strain of American denial about climate change. It appears to be based on a lack of understanding of what climate change is and how it is affecting the planet. For example, polls reveal that a large number of Americans, including the president, are not clear on the difference between climate and weather.

Politics is another factor. Many Republican leaders have chosen to deny the existence of climate change or make light of it. In general, they have fallen in line with President Trump, who has adopted the official stance that climate change is a hoax, despite the overwhelming evidence collected by scientists. Those taking this political position are in the minority, however. According to a 2018 survey by George Mason University's Center for Climate Change Communication, more than half of Americans accept warnings by scientists that climate change is happening. Moreover, 62 percent say they recognize that climate change is mainly caused by human activities. Thus, an ever-growing number of Americans accept the position of the World Wildlife Fund, which stated in 2019,

"Climate change has been verified by almost every nation-state today in some form [and] the science is easily attainable and verified and supported by 97% of climate scientists."[5]

—World Wildlife Fund

Climate change has been verified by almost every nation-state today in some form [and] the science is easily attainable and verified and supported by 97% of climate scientists, with the [deniers] having no single, coherent, and verified alternative theory. . . . Climate change is one of the biggest challenges of our time, and it's our responsibility to tackle it urgently. The time has gone for us to pass this problem onto the next generation. We must face up to this now.[5]

CHAPTER 1

An Onslaught of Extreme Weather Events

Climate change is affecting the planet and human communities in numerous ways, large and small. Of those, the most visible signs of change are episodes of extreme weather and the sometimes-calamitous results of extreme weather conditions. Among them are abnormal heat waves that kill hundreds of people and hospitalize thousands more; massive droughts and disastrous wildfires stoked by those unusually dry conditions; devastating floods that cover hundreds of square miles and cause billions of dollars of damage; and monster hurricanes and other storms driven by rising ocean temperatures. Extreme weather events are causing devastation worldwide. And that, says climate scientist Deepti Singh, "is representative of climate change."[6]

Heat Records Are Continually Broken

As Earth's atmosphere has steadily warmed, heat waves have been happening more often in recent years than in the past several centuries. Around the world, warm days are getting warmer and more frequent. In fact, according to Skeptical Science (a website written by an international team of scientists), record-breaking heat waves are occurring five times more often than they would if human-caused climate change was not involved.

Heat waves are not a new phenomenon; they have occurred off and on throughout the planet's history. When they did occur in the past, however, they tended to be random, localized, and much less frequent than they are now. Also, they were never part of a pattern of consistently rising temperatures over large sectors of the globe, as is the case today. Heat records have been repeatedly broken in many places on the planet in the past few decades and certain years have stood out as extreme. Extreme conditions of this nature occurred in various countries in 1980, 1988, 2003, 2013, and 2018, to name only a few.

Europe suffered a horrendous heat wave in 2003, for instance. For most of the month of August, temperatures hovered daily between 90°F and 100°F (32°C and 38°C) and they soared to 118°F (48°C) in some areas. Europe's hottest summer in five centuries, it caused serious crop failures and forest fires across the continent. In addition, the abnormal heat generated a terrible human death toll. More than twenty thousand people perished in Italy alone, according to Italy's national statistics institute. Nearly every other European nation recorded thousands of heat-related deaths during this same period.

Although the death toll from the 2018 heat event was lower than in 2003, similar temperatures were recorded over a more widespread area in 2018. Los Angeles, California, set new records for high temperatures in July 2018, with consistent readings of 111°F (44°C). On the other side of the world, for the first time in recorded history, areas above the Arctic Circle in Finland experienced temperatures near 90°F (32°C). Overall, May 2018 was the hottest month on record across both Europe and the United States. At the same time, hotter-than-normal temperatures lingered in Canada, Japan, North Africa, Korea, and numerous other parts of the world.

Increasingly Widespread Drought

Climate scientists expect such massive heat events to grow more intense. An outgrowth of these events is the increasing occurrence of large-scale droughts. Dozens of scientific studies have confirmed that droughts began to grow larger and more numerous worldwide during the second half of the twentieth century. Those episodes of unusually dry weather were particularly pronounced in about half a dozen locations.

Among those unusually hard-hit areas have been central and northern Africa and the western United States. The latter recorded increasingly severe drought conditions between 2000 and 2019. Moreover, between 2011 and 2016 one western state, California, underwent its worst sustained drought in recorded history. The year 2018 was especially dry in the southwestern states. The long drought resulted in billions of dollars in crop and livestock losses for farmers. Other impacts have been seen in various western states. NOAA science editor Rebecca Lindsey describes some of those problems:

Endangered fish in the Rio Grande had to be rescued and relocated to wetter stretches as parts of the river in New Mexico dried up. In Arizona and New Mexico, birds and elk have been observed coming to stock ponds and yards for water and food as natural sources of surface water and vegetation become scarce. In Colorado, live-stock operators are hauling water for cows and sheep as stock ponds and streams dry up, and farmers along the Middle Rio Grande in New Mexico have been told to expect half their normal irrigation allotment.[7]

Many thousands of miles to the east, meanwhile, prolonged drought linked by scientists to climate change has adversely affected the lives of tens of millions of people in central Africa. In that region, Lake Chad has long been a major source of drinking water and irrigation for the countries of Chad, Cameroon, Niger, and Nigeria. But the lake is shrinking. During the 1960s, it was the world's sixth-largest lake, with a surface area of over 10,000 square miles (26,000 sq km). The combination of climate change and population growth (leading to increased demand for water) has caused Lake Chad to shrink to less than a tenth its original size. In 2019, only a few hundred square miles of it were left. By then, lack of irrigation water had caused the soil in thousands of surrounding farms to dry out. In turn, crop losses, poverty, and starvation in the area have rapidly increased.

"Endangered fish in the Rio Grande had to be rescued and relocated to wetter stretches as parts of the river in New Mexico dried up."[7]

—NOAA science editor Rebecca Lindsey

Gone in a Single Generation

Among the more dangerous effects of extreme heat events and droughts related to climate change are giant wildfires that destroy both forests and human communities. Long periods of extreme heat and drought—brought about by climate change—have left entire forests and grasslands bone dry and susceptible to devastating blazes that can spread with astonishing speed. Several western US states experienced record numbers of forest and brush fires between 2006 and 2017, and these events reached a terrifying peak in 2018. In California, which had the most numerous as well as the largest fires during these years, the flames scorched thousands of square miles of woodlands and destroyed thousands of homes and businesses.

Of the dozens of big fires that hit California in 2018, the two most severe were the Carr and Camp fires—both of which occurred in the northern part of the state. The Carr fire, which raged during July and August, killed eight people, three of them firefighters. The fire destroyed more than 229,000 acres (92,673 ha) of forest and did an estimated $800 million worth of damage. It also generated a rare secondary weather effect—an enormous tornado-like vortex that scientists call a "firenado." According to

Ranking the Megahurricanes

In light of the increasing number of monster storms that are a product of climate change, the question has arisen: Should scientists add a category 6 to the 1-to-5 scale that measures the strength of hurricanes? Former National Science Foundation member Jeff Nesbit comments on this idea:

> Meteorologists and scientists never imagined that there would be a need for a category 6 storm, with winds that exceed 200 miles per hour [161 kmh] on a sustained basis, sweeping away everything in its path. Until now, such a storm wasn't possible, so there was no need for a new category above category 5. Right now, however, there is anywhere from 5% to 8% more water vapor circulating throughout the atmosphere than there was a generation ago. This, combined with warmer temperatures that are driving water up from the deep ocean in places where hurricanes typically form, has created the potential for superstorms that we haven't seen before and aren't really prepared for. . . . No one in America has ever experienced the wrath and fury of a category 6 hurricane, which now genuinely seems possible and realistic, [and] it's only a matter of time before one hits the US.

Jeff Nesbit, "This Is the Way the World Ends: Will We Soon See Category 6 Hurricanes?," *Guardian*, September 15, 2018. www.theguardian.com.

Neil Lareau, a wildfire expert at the University of Nevada, Reno, it was "one of two scientifically documented cases of that happening. Not only is it extreme, we're talking about events that have only been recorded a handful of times."[8]

As bad as the Carr fire was, for Californians the worst was yet to come. In November 2018 the Camp fire wiped out some 153,000 acres (61,917 ha) and killed at least eighty-six people. So far, the damage estimate has reached $16.5 billion. It was by far the most catastrophic wildfire in California's history up to that time. Gone in a single generation were immense forests that had taken dozens of generations to grow.

The Planet's Giant Heat Engines

Still more climate change–generated extreme weather takes the form of giant ocean storms. In the northern Atlantic and northern Pacific Oceans, these storms are called hurricanes; the same storms are known as typhoons in the western Pacific and as tropical cyclones in the southern Pacific and Indian Oceans.

Whichever name they go by, these weather systems are essentially enormous heat engines. Such a storm is initially generated by the warmth it sucks from the ocean. The warmer the water, the more heat energy it takes in, and that energy drives both the winds themselves and the circular, spinning pattern they form.

Hurricanes have been around for as long as the oceans. What makes the ones that formed in the last several decades different is that they were more intense and destructive thanks to the extra oceanic heat energy directly caused by climate change. Scientists have closely studied these recent storms; a large body of evidence now confirms that, through these storms, climate change has killed thousands of people and caused billions of dollars in damage.

Indeed, since 1970 at least, these storms have been growing larger and more powerful. In 2005, Hurricane Wilma became the strongest Atlantic storm ever recorded. That same year a second giant hurricane, Katrina, struck Louisiana and Mississippi, killing more than eighteen hundred people and causing some $100 billion in property damage. As in the many cases of extreme weather associated with climate change, the warming atmosphere and oceans were not the only factors that caused all that damage. Although scientists have concluded that Katrina was made stronger by climate change, a hefty portion of the damage occurred when human-made levees in Louisiana failed. That failure made the inevitable flooding even worse. Thus, as in this instance, climate change is frequently part of a mix of destructive events.

More than Flukes of Nature

As bad as these two hurricanes were, they were not the only evidence of extreme storms fueled by climate change. More than twenty other even larger hurricanes battered the world between

What was once a busy marina in Lake Mead National Recreation Area in Arizona reveals empty stretches of dry, cracked earth after rising temperatures caused the lake to recede.

2006 and 2019. One of the worst hurricanes was Matthew, which struck Haiti and the southeastern United States in 2016. It killed 603 people and caused $15 billion in damage; still worse was Hurricane Maria in 2017, which killed at least 3,057 people in Puerto Rico and caused a whopping $92 billion in damage. Two other hurricanes, Florence and Michael, both occurred in 2018. Michael was the strongest hurricane in recorded history to make landfall on the Florida Panhandle. In the Pacific in 2018, Yutu, Mangkhut, and five other bigger-than-normal typhoons smashed into coastlines, killing 771 people and causing more than $18 billion in damage.

Climate scientists agree that this unprecedented series of giant storms would not have been so numerous if not for the on-

Harsher Winters Do Not Disprove Climate Change

Republican senator Jim Inhofe of Oklahoma is a staunch climate change denier. In 2015 Inhofe carried a large snowball onto the Senate floor to show that climate change is a hoax. It was freezing outside that day in Washington, DC, Inhofe pointed out. If global warming was real, he said, it should be warmer in winter, not colder.

Far from demonstrating that climate change is not happening, the senator's action merely showed that he misunderstands the science of climate change. That science does not predict that warm weather will prevail everywhere on the planet. Rather, there are and will continue to be vast weather extremes, including colder-than-average temperatures in some places. This is partly because Earth's steadily warming atmosphere has increasingly disturbed the polar vortex, the mass of frigid air that straddles the Arctic region. Normally that air rarely dips southward. However, in recent decades the pressure of warm air on the vortex's boundaries has caused the jet stream to take wild swings, carrying freezing air southward into the United States.

Another reason why climate change brings colder weather to some places is because the warming atmosphere holds more water vapor. The extra water periodically falls to the earth as precipitation. In lower altitudes, that moisture takes the form of rain; but in higher altitudes, where it is naturally colder, it falls as snow. Thus, some higher-altitude regions can and do get more snow as a result of climate change.

going phenomenon of climate change. Nor would they have struck with such force. Many were category 5 storms, each featuring sustained winds of up to 200 miles per hour (322 kmh). On the intensity scale that scientists employ to measure such events, category 1 storms are the mildest, and category 5 storms are the most violent.

Moreover, this increase in the intensity of big ocean storms will likely continue in the coming decades. As the Union of Concerned Scientists notes, "The projected increase in intense hurricanes is substantial—a doubling or more in the frequency of category 4 and 5 storms by the end of the century—with the western North Atlantic experiencing the largest increase."[9]

Thousand-Year Floods Are Increasingly Common

Coastal communities are not the only areas that suffer from the devastation wrought by hurricanes. As one of those huge storms moves inland, it dumps vast amounts of rain on dozens and sometimes hundreds of cities and towns that lie in its path. That adds to large flooding events caused primarily by the increased amounts of water vapor in the steadily warming atmosphere. Freakish clusters of extremely heavy rainstorms used to occur once every twenty to thirty years on average; but they now happen every one to three years across large sections of the globe.

In the United States alone, statistics show that large floods increased considerably in number and intensity from 1959 to 2019, with the biggest increases happening from the late 1990s on. In addition to thousands of deaths, those floods have caused well over $20 billion in crop and property damage since the 1960s. In 2013, a so-called thousand-year rainfall event struck the Colorado Rockies, setting off terrible flash floods and mudslides in the Boulder area and in some of Denver's suburbs.

A partially submerged playground is visible in Bellevue, Kentucky, shortly after torrential rains caused the Ohio River to crest to an astounding 60.5 feet on February 25, 2018.

Overall, the hardest-hit US regions have been the ones containing complex giant river systems, especially those of the Mississippi and Ohio Rivers. With so much water already flowing through such areas, extreme rainfall events inevitably cause them to flood. According to experts interviewed in 2017 by Kentucky's largest newspaper, the *Courier-Journal,* the many rivers and streams making up the Ohio River system have been in crisis mode due to frequent large climate change–driven floods. Climate change, they say, is pushing "the Ohio River and its tributaries into uncharted waters." This is "setting off economic and environmental crises like never before across a 13-state region."[10]

The paper's reporters also interviewed members of the US Army Corps of Engineers, who have struggled to avert total disaster in the region. Kathleen D. White, a climate change expert with the corps, explained that flooding and power failures are becoming ever more frequent in Kentucky, Indiana, and the rest of the Ohio River basin. "The changes are happening today," she emphasizes. "This isn't something that's just in the future."[11]

The same thing is happening in a number of other countries. In 2018 historic Florence, Italy, experienced its worst flooding in decades; in Kerala, India, meanwhile, hundreds died and thousands became homeless during multiple, devastating thousand-year floods. The year 2018 also brought the biggest flash floods in over a century to France's Aude River.

> "The [climatic] changes are happening today. This isn't something that's just in the future."[11]
>
> —Kathleen D. White, a climate scientist with the US Army Corps of Engineers

The New Normal

Such massive flooding events, along with destructive heat waves, droughts, wildfires, and hurricanes, have already become the new normal, scientists warn. Moreover, the connection between this abnormal activity and climate change has been firmly established. As a December 2018 report by the American Meteorological Society stated, "Scientific evidence supports increasing confidence that human activity is driving a variety of extreme events now. These are having large economic impacts across the United States and around the world."[12]

The natural world is changing. "Nature is increasingly rolling back its curtain of sensitivity to rising greenhouse gases,"[13] says Martin Hoerling, a NOAA research scientist. One result of that heightened sensitivity is a growing frequency and intensity of all sorts of extreme weather events. And these events are likely to continue, scientists warn, unless and until the world's people change how they live.

CHAPTER 2

The Ongoing Threat of Sea-Level Rise

One of the most far-reaching effects of climate change is rising sea levels across the globe. Water level in the planet's oceans has never been constant. Scientists have found evidence that the seas have risen and fallen by differing amounts many times during Earth's 4.6-billion-year history. Thus, the phenomenon is not new.

The difference between past episodes of sea-level rise and what is occurring now can be summed up in a single word: rapidity. The ancient examples of changing ocean levels, which had various natural causes, almost always occurred very slowly—often just a fraction of an inch per century. In contrast, during the past few decades, the rate has sped up considerably. Scientists say this is due, in large part, to a warming atmosphere caused by the burning of fossil fuels (coal, oil, and natural gas). The rate of sea-level rise is now roughly 0.1 inch (0.25 cm) per year and is still accelerating. Between 1993 and 2017 alone, average global sea levels rose more than 3 inches (7.6 cm).

A rise in sea level of a few inches may not sound like much. But scientists know that enormous amounts of extra water are needed to cause such a change. That surplus water inevitably creeps up onto land surfaces and thereby alters coastlines around the world.

Moreover, the expansion of the oceans is speeding up, fueled by two principal processes. The first is called thermal expansion. As the overriding global climate continues to warm, the seas absorb some of that warmth. As a common science class experiment shows, when someone heats a beaker of water, the volume of that liquid expands. That same process is presently taking place on a much larger scale in Earth's oceans. The second, and even more consequential cause of sea-level rise, is the steady melting of glaciers and the ice packs covering most of the Arctic and Antarctic regions and Greenland.

Disappearing Glaciers

For instance, glaciers around the world that remained about the same size for tens or hundreds of thousands of years have recently been melting at alarming rates. Daniel Fagre of the US Geological Survey's Global Change Research Program has long been studying the retreating glaciers in Montana's Glacier National Park. When the park was created in 1910, he says, it had at least 150 glaciers. There are now fewer than thirty, and most of the remaining ones are a third of their original size. "Things that normally happen in geologic time [millions of years] are happening during the span of a human lifetime," Fagre explains. "It's like watching the Statue of Liberty melt."[14]

Glaciers and other similar ice packs in other parts of the world have been disappearing at similar rates. Among the better-known examples are the glaciers that sit atop Africa's highest peak, the towering volcano Mount Kilimanjaro. After hundreds of centuries of existence, these ice packs have thawed and evaporated by more than 80 percent since 1912. Similarly, the many glaciers in northern India are vanishing at astonishing rates. At this pace, most of the glaciers in the central and eastern Himalayas may be gone by as soon as 2035 or 2040. Glaciers in the higher elevations of Peru, Switzerland, Indonesia, and the huge frozen island of Greenland are receding as well.

Scientists have been keeping a close eye on these developments for decades. In fact, one of the most important predictors of the effects of climate change is the ongoing shrinkage of the world's glaciers. Experts measure the size of such ice packs in units called gigatons, with each gigaton equaling 1 billion tons.

Rainbow Mountain in the Andes mountain range in Peru (pictured) used to be completely covered by snow. Climate change has caused the local snowpack to substantially diminish.

They found that the loss of glacier mass accelerated from 226 gigatons per year worldwide during the 1970s and 1980s to 275 gigatons per year after 1993.

By 2019, the rate of loss was up to 335 gigatons per year. This is the finding of a special research team from Switzerland's University of Zurich. The team, led by Michael Zemp, found that the planet has lost 9,000 gigatons, or 9 trillion tons, of ice from glaciers since 1961. "In other words," Zemp explains, "every single year we are losing about three times the volume of all ice stored in the European Alps, and this accounts for around 30 percent of the current rate of sea-level rise."[15]

Arctic Ice Losses

Meanwhile, the conversion of ice to seawater from the Arctic and Antarctic regions has been expanding in scope at an alarming rate. Clear-cut evidence indicates that between 1989 and 2019, the Arctic ice sheets lost at least 10 percent of their volume. Before the advent of the Industrial Revolution some two centuries ago, that volume had remained roughly the same for hundreds of thousands of years. The National Snow and Ice Data Center (NSIDC) in Boulder, Colorado, gives some specific figures: "Arctic sea ice extent for April 2019 averaged 5.19 million square miles (13.45 million sq. km). This was 479,000 square miles (1.24 million sq. km) below the 1981 to 2010 long-term average extent and 89,000 square miles (230,000 sq. km) below the previous record low set in April 2016."[16]

Even more disturbing than the overall Arctic ice loss is the *kind* of ice that has melted the fastest. Scientists divide the ice in the Arctic and Antarctic into two main categories—old ice, which has built up over four, five, or more years; and new ice, laid down in the past year or two. Old ice is thicker and more durable than new ice, which is much more susceptible to rapid melting. The NSIDC reports that "nearly all of the oldest ice, which once made up around 30 percent of the sea ice within the Arctic Ocean, is gone. As of mid-April 2019, the [old] ice made up only 1.2 percent of the ice cover."[17]

"Nearly all of the oldest ice, which once made up around 30 percent of the sea ice within the Arctic Ocean, is gone."[17]

—National Snow and Ice Data Center

These massive reductions in the size of the Arctic ice sheets have contributed to ongoing rises in global sea levels. Climate scientists and geologists say that the rate of sea-level rise during the twentieth and twenty-first centuries was far higher than in any of the past twenty-eight centuries. Moreover, about half of the observed rise happened between 1993 and 2019.

Shattering Ice Shelves

In the Antarctic, ice is melting at an even faster rate. Ice loss more than quadrupled, from 30 gigatons per year during the 1990s to 147 gigatons per year by 2011. The rate of loss continued to accelerate between 2011 and 2019. Furthermore, such ice losses in the Antarctic frequently occur in the form of sudden, dramatic breakups of the region's monstrous ice shelves. Unlike the Arctic ice cap, which is composed mainly of frozen water, Antarctica is a continental landmass that came to be covered with snow and ice.

Over geologic time, large glaciers and other ice formations slowly moved across Antarctica's land buried deep below. Creeping along at the rate of only a few inches per year, these giant ice rivers eventually reached the coasts; there, they became enormous floating ice shelves that still cling to the continent. These ice shelves have remained in place for thousands of years. Today, however, pieces of these shelves are fracturing and slipping away into the ocean at an ever-increasing rate.

One of the largest and most memorable examples of this remarkable process occurred in March 2002. Photos taken by satellites showed the sudden and violent disintegration of an immense portion of the so-called Larsen B ice shelf. In the biggest example of such an event ever witnessed by humans, more than 1,255 square miles (3,250 sq km) of the shelf broke up into hundreds of free-floating icebergs. The shattering process—the undoing of an estimated twelve thousand years of slow, steady formation—took a mere thirty-five days. The icebergs drifted away and dissolved into the ocean, leaving behind a newly created bay on the Antarctic coastline.

This fragmentation process continues. Not long after the March 2002 incident, the remaining section of Larsen B lost another 656 square miles (1,700 sq km) of ice. Much of that later breakup consisted of the creation of a massive new free-floating iceberg in 2006.

What is more, the loss of these gigantic chunks of the ice shelf re-

"When an ice shelf disintegrates, glaciers behind it accelerate abruptly, and begin to draw down significant volumes of ice and put it into the ocean."[18]

—Ted Scambos, an expert on glaciers

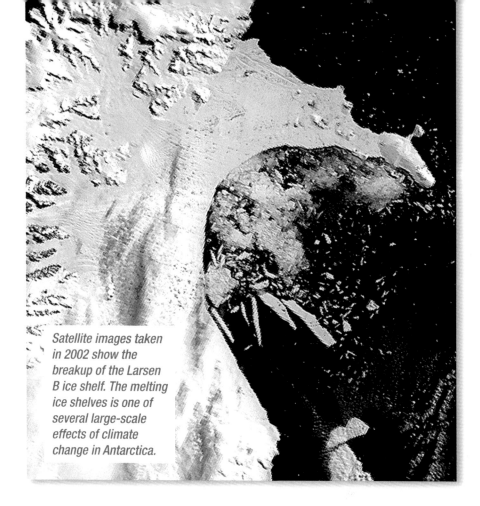

Satellite images taken in 2002 show the breakup of the Larsen B ice shelf. The melting ice shelves is one of several large-scale effects of climate change in Antarctica.

leased a lot of the pressure that had been holding back glaciers farther inland. As a result, these ice sheets are moving toward the ocean at an accelerated rate. As NSIDC researcher and noted glacier expert Ted Scambos explains, "In both Greenland and Antarctica we're seeing over and over again that when an ice shelf disintegrates, glaciers behind it accelerate abruptly, and begin to draw down significant volumes of ice and put it into the ocean."[18]

Not only have these events already significantly raised global sea levels, but they have also created the real potential for further destabilization of the Antarctic ice shelves. That scenario is a clear recipe for disaster. "The Larsen B shelf was about the size of Connecticut," says science writer Laura Naranjo. "But Antarctica's largest ice shelves, the Ross and Ronne, are each nearly

The Ocean Encroaches in Chesapeake Bay

Parts of Gloucester County, located in Virginia's Chesapeake Bay region, are among the areas of the eastern United States that are already threatened by rising sea levels. Sections of the county that used to be dry and rarely experienced flooding are now either soggy and marshy or completely under water. "The challenges are really great," says Lewis Lawrence, the executive director of the Middle Peninsula Planning District Commission, which is trying to deal with the problems associated with the encroaching ocean. "We've got more water than we know what to do with," he adds. The commission has been working with the Virginia Institute of Marine Science to map out the likely physical challenges that roads and buildings in Gloucester County will experience in the decades ahead.

Christy Miller Hesed of the University of Maryland has also been studying Gloucester County's plight. The situation is becoming increasingly serious for many property owners in the region. "There are going to be marshes migrating inland all around the Chesapeake Bay," Hesed predicts. "For a lot of property owners in these rural areas, they're the last generation that's going to live there. Their kids have moved elsewhere. They're not going to be able to sell their property because property values have plummeted." Lawrence, Hesed, and the other local experts hope to find ways to buy these affected residents a little more time before the sea totally claims their lands.

Quoted in Tamara Dietrich, "Rural Coastal Residents Overlooked in Sea Level Rise Impacts, Solutions," *Daily Press,* February 22, 2019. www.dailypress.com.

the size of Spain. If the Ross shelf collapsed, for example, the resulting flow of glacial ice could eventually raise global sea level by up to 16 feet (5 m)."[19]

Why Sea-Level Rise Is a Danger

If everyone in the world lived far from the coasts, rising ocean levels might not be a problem. However, the reality is that many of the world's largest and most economically important cities, along with other densely populated areas, lie right on seacoasts. In the United States, for instance, nearly 40 percent of Americans dwell in exposed coastal areas. Here, the term *exposed* applies to places where sea level has an established role in local flooding, beach and marsh erosion, and potentially severe damage from major storms.

On a global scale, more than half of the world's ten biggest cities are located on or near seacoasts. Many of these cities have already experienced street and sewer flooding during large storms. Bridges, subway systems, freshwater reservoirs, power plants, landfills, and other large-scale examples of traditional, vital infrastructure are also susceptible to flooding and costly damage. In turn, the jobs of the many people who work in these facilities are at increasing risk.

Some local economies are already feeling the pinch as they have sunk millions of dollars into beefing up seawalls and other makeshift barriers to the rising oceans. NOAA has documented numerous examples of what it calls "nuisance flooding," a preliminary version of the larger climate change–generated floods to come. During nuisance flooding, a NOAA article states,

"If the Ross [ice] shelf collapsed . . . the resulting flow of glacial ice could eventually raise global sea level by up to 16 feet (5 m)."[19]

—Science writer Laura Naranjo

waves may overtop old seawalls, water may inundate low-lying roads, and storm-water drainage can be diminished. These impacts may not be life threatening, but they disrupt transportation, damage infrastructure, and strain city and county maintenance budgets. A nuisance flood can become a more severe problem if a local rainstorm, storm surge, or wave-overtopping event coincides with high tide.[20]

Nuisance flooding used to be a fairly rare occurrence. But due to climate change, officials in coastal areas of Massachusetts, New Jersey, Maryland, North Carolina, California, Hawaii, and some other states have reported steadily increasing incidents in recent years. Nuisance floods are not only expensive to clean up, but they also make local underground water levels higher. So, when large hurricanes like Katrina and Michael strike, their flood-waters are not absorbed locally as much as they were in prior decades. Therefore, the major floodwaters tend to push further inland than in the past. Nuisance flooding and floods from big storms—both made worse by rising sea levels—also increasingly stress coastal ecosystems that harbor wildlife and fish, including commercial fisheries.

Cities in Trouble

Some cities around the globe are already suffering more than nuisance flooding and are struggling to repel the considerably larger, more costly effects of sea-level rise. One well-known example in the United States is Miami, one of Florida's most popular vacation destinations. Hardest hit so far in the area is Miami Beach, which lies on a long, narrow island running parallel to the city of Miami.

The streets of Dhaka, Bangladesh, are submerged in rising water after heavy rains in 2017. Millions of people in the city were severely affected by rising tides.

A Climate Change Skeptic Weighs In

At least 95 percent of climate scientists now accept that the present onslaught of climate change is primarily caused by human activities, says John Cook, a professor at the Center for Climate Change Communication at George Mason University. Cook also notes that over 97 percent of recent scientific papers on climate change agree with that position. However, a few reputable scientists do dissent to one degree or another. They call themselves climate change skeptics (as opposed to climate change deniers). The skeptics agree that the planet's atmosphere is warming, but they disagree that human activities are the main cause of that warming.

One noted skeptic is William Happer, a former Princeton University physics professor and current member of President Trump's National Security Council. Happer has said that he doubts that human production of carbon dioxide has had much influence on global temperatures. "All the evidence I see is that the current warming of the climate is just like past warmings," he has stated previously. "In fact, it's not as much as past warmings yet, and it probably has little to do with carbon dioxide."

Through his many years of study, Happer has become "convinced that the current alarm over carbon dioxide is mistaken." It is his belief that there is some-thing that is making Earth's atmosphere warmer that scientists "still don't really understand."

Quoted in *Daily Princetonian*, "Professor Denies Global Warming Theory," 2009. www.dailyprince tonian.com.

Each year in the decade preceding 2018, tidal surges battered Miami Beach's west coast. Excess seawater poured into the local storm drains and overloaded them, causing progressively worse street flooding. Robin McKie, a reporter for the *Guardian,* writes, "The effect is calamitous. Shops and houses are inundated; city life is paralyzed; cars are ruined by the corrosive seawater that immerses them."[21] The city tried to stop these damaging floods by improving Miami Beach's hard-hit system of drains and sewers. Altogether, city officials have invested about $1.5 billion in projects intended to hold back the rising waters.

A smaller American town is also desperately attempting to fight the effects of rising ocean levels. Newtok, on Alaska's northwestern coast, is struggling to survive. As the surrounding sea steadily rises, each year at least 70 feet (21 m) of the land on which the town rests disappears forever beneath the waves. In 2018 the US Congress allotted $15 million to relocate some of the local population of several hundred people to higher inland regions. It quickly became clear, however, that that amount of money was too small to relocate everyone. Therefore, town officials are urgently looking elsewhere for more money.

Similar stories can be found around the world. For instance, as rising tides and giant storms engulf large sections of Bangladesh, millions of people have already fled to the country's capital, Dhaka. The fastest-growing large city in the world, Dhaka's population now tops 18 million. Almost 7 million of those inhabitants live in dire conditions. The International Organization for Migration points out that 70 percent of them were driven into poverty by rising waters caused by climate change. As *CR Magazine*'s Mary Mazzoni puts it,

> While some still view climate change as some distant or unidentifiable threat (and others simply argue its effects "won't be so bad"), the impacts of rising tides and surging temperatures are already changing lives around the world. From South Florida to the Pacific Islands, this list represents thousands of lives that are forever altered by the warming climate—and a threat to millions more unless something changes quickly.[22]

CHAPTER 3

Climate Change and Global Food Supply

Between 2019 and 2050, the world's population will grow by more than 3 billion people, climbing to a total of nearly 10 billion. With all those extra mouths to feed, the global community will face daunting challenges. In part, this will be due to the effects of climate change; yet even now, increasing atmospheric and ocean temperatures are making it increasingly difficult to feed all of the planet's inhabitants.

A major reason for this growing predicament is that agricultural areas around the globe are progressively feeling the physical stress caused by extreme heat and drought. The prestigious National Academy of Sciences calculates that each degree Celsius of planetary warming leads to an average of 10 percent loss of present crop yields. This translates into a serious threat to large-scale food availability and, in turn, human health. Climate change–related instability in the global food system is already being felt in major food-growing regions of the United States, reports Columbia University's Center for Climate and Life:

In the United States, the 2012 summer heat wave and drought in the Midwest—where corn alone is a multibillion-dollar industry—led to a massive drop in crop yields, while the . . . drought in California . . . [was] causing large-scale transformation of agriculture in this leading fruit-, vegetable- and nut-producing state. Because food is a globally traded commodity, climate events in one part of the world can raise prices and limit consumption far afield.[23]

The Effects of Drought and Groundwater Depletion

Making these ongoing drought-driven threats to food more complex and thereby harder to combat is the fact that food production methods differ from region to region. About 80 percent of the world's crops are rain fed; moreover, the lands they grow on are distributed randomly around the globe. Crop production in those areas depends on complicated but normally predictable weather patterns that bring needed moisture at specific times of the year.

The problem is that climate change is steadily altering and randomizing those weather patterns. First, periodic, abnormally long, and hot droughts cause needed rains to arrive too late or too early. Also, the warming atmosphere holds more water than it did in past eras. So, when the rains do finally fall on fields that have been parched by drought, the precipitation can be so in-

In August 2013, the long-term effects of drought were evident in cornfields outside of Navasota, Texas. Climate change has frequently made existing droughts more severe.

tense that it washes away much of the good soil. In addition, such minifloods frequently carry sewage, manure, and/or pollutants from farms, lawns, roads, and landfills. This introduces toxins and disease-causing germs into the food supply.

One important rain-fed crop that is already feeling these adverse effects is rice, which is popular worldwide but is a major staple in Asia. In recent years dry periods have increased in number and severity in southern Asia. The result has been decreases of 17 to 40 percent in rain-fed rice yields in most years. One particularly hard-hit region is the Ping River Basin in northern Thailand. Agriculture is the most important economic activity in that nation, accounting for about 25 percent of its gross national product and a whopping 60 percent of total exports. Yet the Ping River Basin, one of Thailand's prime rice-growing areas, has experienced climate-related rice crop losses as high as 55 percent in recent years, according to the *Journal of Earth Science and Climate Change*.

In the United States and a number of other nations, the wine-making industry is also suffering from the effects of climate change. According to the global company Acciona, which promotes renewable energy sources,

> The best vintages [of wine grapes] usually arise during the seasons in which springs are very rainy and summers are warm, since this accelerates the ripening of the grape allowing early wines of quality to be obtained. However, changes in the atmospheric conditions and the gradual rise in temperatures are causing alterations in the vineyards which affect the production of wine.[24]

Such changes in growing cycles cause many varieties of grapes to ripen poorly, which seriously reduces the quality of the resulting wines. In other cases, vineyards have been devastated

How Scientists Study Climate Change

The prestigious National Centre for Atmospheric Science in the United Kingdom explains the three primary methods scientists employ to gather and interpret data about climate change:

Observing climate. Scientists call any measurement of the state of the Earth an observation. For climate, important observations include records of rainfall amounts, images of the Earth from space, surface pressure readings, measurements from ocean buoys, and many other things. Averaging and other processing of the observations gives us a record of long-term climate [and] how climate has changed over time. . . .

Understanding climate. Using observations and simulations, scientists piece together an understanding of how the climate system works. For example, we know that clouds, which are made up of water droplets, absorb and re-emit heat released by the surface of the Earth, acting like a blanket. One familiar effect of this is that cloudy nights are considerably warmer than clear nights. This effect can be observed and quantified, and the knowledge is then used to test and improve climate simulations.

Simulating climate. Climate simulators (also known as climate models) are complex computer programs designed to solve mathematical equations which describe the behavior of the Earth's climate system. . . . These equations are solved by running computer programs on very powerful supercomputers which carry out the many millions of calculations needed. Climate simulators are tested against observations of the real climate system [and] they can simulate many aspects of climate and its variability and are being continuously improved.

National Centre for Atmospheric Science, "How Do NCAS-Climate Scientists Study Climate?" www.ncas.ac.uk.

by droughts. Others have been ravaged by giant climate change–driven wildfires. A number of California's prime vineyards were badly damaged by wildfires between 2017 and 2019.

Meanwhile, of the 20 percent of global crops that are grown using groundwater, fully half come from regions where that precious liquid is not renewable. This happens because underground aquifers are draining faster than they are refilling. The situation is steadily worsening as the atmosphere continues to warm because droughts are occurring more often and the resulting loss of rainfall contributes to dwindling underground water supplies. The negative effects of this process can already be seen in large crop-producing areas in the US Great Plains, California's Central Valley, northeastern China, India, Pakistan, and some sections of Iraq and Iran. "Groundwater depletion is a slow-building pressure on our food system," says Columbia University scientist Michael Puma. "And we don't have any effective policies in place to deal with the fact that we are depleting our major resources in our major food producing regions, which is pretty disconcerting."[25]

The Warming World and Livestock

Livestock of various kinds constitutes another food-producing resource that is adversely affected by steadily rising global atmospheric temperatures. A number of domesticated animals become less fertile and more vulnerable to disease in hot weather. Dairy cows, for example, are particularly sensitive to warm temperatures, and keeping them cool in spring and summer has become a major challenge for dairy farmers in recent years. As Cassandra Tucker, an animal science professor at the University of California, Davis, and her colleagues explain,

> When cows get too hot, their milk production decreases. Severe overheating can threaten cows' health and their ability to get pregnant and carry calves to term. Dairy farmers use fans and sprayers to cool cows in their barns, but there is a substantial need for better options. Existing systems use a lot of energy and water, which is costly for farmers. And climate change is raising temperatures and stressing California's water supplies.[26]

Another livestock-related problem is that the world's growing human population requires more and more meat from cattle, sheep, chickens, and other farm animals every year. About 56 billion land animals are raised and slaughtered for human consumption annually. That figure is expected to double by 2050.

Biologists and other experts point out that at the same time that humans need to raise more farm animals for food, those very increases in livestock numbers are worsening climate change. This occurs because raising livestock produces large amounts of greenhouse gases. First, the farming industry burns enormous amounts of fossil fuels to make the fertilizers needed to grow soy beans and other crops those animals eat. Accord-

In 2006 a record-setting heat wave killed thousands of cows in California. This dairy farm in Kerman uses fans and sprinklers to keep its livestock cool.

Maple Syrup Losses

One of the many food-related industries facing challenges caused by the warming atmosphere is maple syrup production, known in the business as *sugar making.* Its problems are most acute in Canada, which generates 70 percent of the world's maple syrup. In 2012, for example, the Canadian sugar-making industry's output of syrup fell by 54 percent in the province of Ontario and by 12.5 percent in Canada as a whole.

Successful sugar making relies on specific temperature conditions, including daytime highs above freezing and nighttime lows below freezing. This usually occurs as winter turns to spring, and fall into winter. These conditions allow the flow of sap, a thick liquid that the farmers boil to create maple syrup. In the past, sugar makers had six to eight weeks in which those ideal temperatures prevailed and the sap could be extracted from the trees. But climate change has reduced that productive period to as little as two weeks in several parts of Canada. It has also affected US maple producers. Some have been forced to tap trees earlier than in the past. "I'm in my 60s," says Helen Thomas, a New York maple producer. "When I was a kid, my dad had the rule that you tapped around March 15." In contrast, Thomas and other maple farmers now tap in late January. In the short run, climate change is already making existing supplies of syrup more expensive. But industry experts worry that if atmospheric warming continues, real maple syrup could become a rare and costly commodity.

Quoted in Kendra Pierre-Louis, "Syrup Is as Canadian as a Maple Leaf. That Could Change with the Climate," *New York Times*, May 3, 2019. www.nytimes.com.

ing to Yale University scholar James E. McWilliams, that burning alone generates roughly 41 million metric tons of the greenhouse gas carbon dioxide annually. Also, the billions of cows and other meat-producing animals raised each year release an estimated 86 million metric tons of the potent greenhouse gas methane when they pass gas. No nation or group of nations has yet even attempted to solve these problems on a large scale.

Fish in the Warming Oceans

Land animals are not the only major source of protein for the burgeoning human population. Close to 600 million people around the globe get the bulk of their protein from fish and other sea creatures, and more than 2 billion more consume seafood at least sometimes. The principal challenge in this regard is that since the 1950s, the oceans have absorbed a large proportion of the surplus warmth trapped in the atmosphere by greenhouse gas emissions. The result is that the seas are now noticeably warmer than they were in 1880, when scientists first started measuring their temperature.

"Those rising temperatures are creating an epic underwater refugee crisis among marine life,"[27] states a Reuters news service report that details the effects of climate change on the oceans between 2015 and 2019. The findings of the Reuters investigation reflect the conclusions of similar scientific studies. Researchers have found that many species of fish and shellfish try to avoid the warmth by moving northward into regions with cooler waters. "Fish are like Goldilocks," quips Rutgers University biologist Malin L. Pinsky. "They don't like their water too hot or too cold."[28]

> "Fish are like Goldilocks. They don't like their water too hot or too cold."[28]
>
> —Rutgers University biologist Malin L. Pinsky

For instance, until the late 1970s and early 1980s, fishermen routinely caught large numbers of summer flounder off the coast of North Carolina. By 2010 or so, however, most of the summer flounder that had frequented those waters had moved farther up the Eastern Seaboard. During the same period, black sea bass, red hake, and several other fish species that long frequented the middle of the Eastern Seaboard shifted their main habitat some 120 miles (193 km) northward.

Meanwhile, before the 1980s, only about 50 percent of the lobsters caught by US fishermen inhabited the waters along the coast of Maine. The rest came from more southerly coastal regions, where the water temperature was still reasonably cold. But due to increased ocean warming during the relatively few decades that followed, many lobsters migrated northward. By 2019, around 85 percent of US lobsters were captured off Maine's coast.

The same sort of situation has transpired on the West Coast. For dozens of human generations, Chinook salmon were plentiful in the rivers and coastal waters of Northern California and Oregon. Many of those fish migrated northward during the last few decades, however, and are now moving into colder Arctic rivers.

The Negative Effects of Marine Migrations

At first glance, it might seem that the northward shift of many fish and other ocean species would not be very disruptive or harmful. After all, fishermen could simply deploy their nets and traps in different regions. The reality of the situation, however, is not nearly that simple or that benign. First, sea creatures that migrate into new areas often encounter competition with other local species over habitat and especially food. A certain proportion of the fish of a given species do not survive this life-and-death contest.

Also, these northward migrations usually do not happen all at once. Rather, several generations of a fish species will be born and die off while most of the general population travels to suitably cooler waters. During those interim generations, babies are born and live out their lives in water that is somewhat warmer than what is ideal for them. This, biologists point out, can subtly alter their reproduction patterns and speed up their metabolism, which is the process of digesting nutrients.

Some studies indicate that one result of that more rapid metabolism is the absorption of more mercury and other heavy metals. These substances are part of the pollution released during industrial processes (including the burning of fossil fuels) that ends up in the oceans. When humans consume the contaminated fish, they take in those substances, which have harmful effects on human health.

The slightly higher water temperatures that the creatures are exposed to during their migrations can also increase the incidence of marine diseases. Diseases of all kinds, whether marine or not, thrive in warmer temperatures. Such pathogens, like heavy metals and other toxins, can pass through the food chain from sea creatures to humans. For example, the *Vibrio* bacterium, which is known to infect shellfish, can be absorbed by a person who eats those shellfish.

Northward marine migrations have other drawbacks, including creating difficulties for fishermen. Some of them must take their boats much farther from home than they did in the past, which means longer work hours. Also, when far from home, those fishermen often have to adjust to different rules that regulate the industry in various local regions. They may no longer be allowed to catch some of the species that they and their parents and grandparents traditionally caught. "The fish are moving, and the regulations have got to move with the fish,"[29] says sixty-two-year-old Bobby Guzzo, a lifelong fisherman based in Stonington, Connecticut. These factors already negatively affect the livelihoods of thousands of fishermen like Guzzo.

Smaller Catches

Warming seas have had another effect on fish and other marine creatures in recent decades. Several ocean-dwelling species—whether they migrate or not—have reacted to higher water temperatures by producing fewer offspring. As a result, fishermen have experienced smaller overall catches of various species than was common in the past.

In some cases, these reductions in numbers have been substantial. In the Sea of Japan and in the northeastern Atlantic Ocean, for instance, fish populations have diminished as much as 35 percent since the 1930s. In addition, the areas where water has warmed the most have often been overfished by companies and individuals trying to make up for financial losses incurred by the northward migrations. This practice has further reduced catches and has damaged the existing ecosystems. According to Pinsky, "When a fish colonizes a new region, those populations are especially vulnerable to overfishing. That really has serious consequences for the food we can get out of the ocean, the nutrition and the jobs that are supplied."[30]

Avoiding overfishing and using more efficient fishing methods can help reverse a small proportion of those damages. But by themselves they are not nearly enough. *New York Times* climate expert Kendra Pierre-Louis points out that, as in the cases of reduced global crop yields and problems raising livestock, ultimately "the solution lies in slowing or halting climate change."[31]

CHAPTER 4

Ongoing Losses of Species and Biodiversity

Roughly 1 million animal and plant species are presently in danger of extinction. That includes about 40 percent of amphibian species and a third of all marine mammals. More than half a million of these endangered species already lack the habitats they would require for long-term survival. Thus, many of them are likely doomed to disappear in the next few years and cannot be saved.

These dire facts are among the findings of a long-term United Nations (UN) scientific study reported in 2019. Called the Intergovernmental Science-Policy Platform on Biodiversity and Ecosystem Services (IPBES), it was conducted by an international panel of distinguished biologists and other scientists. They examined the present state of the animal and plant kingdoms worldwide and determined which species are threatened with extinction and which are still stable and safe.

The report concluded that a million plant and animal species are threatened with annihilation, and human beings are most to blame for this state of affairs. In fact, the scientists found, human activities have already driven numerous species to extinction in recent times. This corroborates similar recent scientific studies, including one reported in 2018 by the World Wildlife Fund (WWF), which showed that humans have wiped out an incredible 60 percent of bird, fish, reptile, and mammal species since 1970.

The human activities named in these studies include, among others, overfishing; polluting the environment with chemicals and other toxins; massive deforestation, or loss of forests, by burning them; and the direct burning of fossil fuels in factories, cars, and so forth. The latter two share a connection to climate change. The direct burning of fossil fuels is the leading cause of climate change. Deforestation by burning is the second most prevalent cause of global greenhouse gas emissions and thereby another major driver of climate change.

> "We are eroding the very foundations of our economies, livelihoods, food security, health and quality of life worldwide."[32]
>
> —Robert Watson, chairman of the 2019 UN report on global biodiversity

This overall assault on nature has disrupted countless global ecosystems. "We are eroding the very foundations of our economies, livelihoods, food security, health and quality of life worldwide,"[32] says Robert Watson, the IPBES chairperson. His colleague in the study, Josef Settele, agrees. "The essential, interconnected web of life on Earth is getting smaller and increasingly frayed," he says. This "constitutes a direct threat to human wellbeing in all regions of the world."[33]

Ecosystems in a Delicate Balance

The loss of thousands of species is not easily remedied. As Watson explains, the various plant and animal ecosystems across the natural world have long been locked in a delicate balance, with some plant ecosystems supporting animals and vice versa. Experts refer to this vast variety of life forms and their complex interactions as *biodiversity*. Because people themselves steadily evolved within this biodiverse network of ecosystems, that network is in numerous ways vital to human life. "Nature contributes to human wellbeing culturally and spiritually, as well as through the critical production of food, clean water, and energy, and through regulating the Earth's climate, pollution, pollination, and floods,"[34] says Watson.

Examples abound of how the biodiverse planetary network of ecosystems works for the benefit of all involved. Perhaps the most obvious illustration is how green plants take in carbon dioxide and then produce oxygen through the process of photosynthesis. Land animals, including humans, breathe oxygen. That means that green-plant ecosystems are essential for the life-giving respiration of people, dogs, cattle, birds, and other animals. Without a proper supply of green plants, oxygen levels would fall below the level required to support humanity.

Similarly, bees and certain other insects pollinate the plants that produce fruits, nuts, and a wide range of other foodstuffs. If those insects become extinct, pollination will halt and major human food sources will disappear. Coral reefs, which lie along many coastlines, are another example. These reefs provide habitats for thousands of marine species that would die without them. On some coasts, coral reefs, along with mangrove swamps, provide protection from large sea waves as well. Many more people and

A portion of the Great Barrier Reef, off the coast of Australia, is visible in this photo. Between 2014 and 2018, a severe heat wave badly damaged more than two-thirds of the reef.

animals would die during hurricanes and tsunamis without these natural protections.

Still another example involves two land creatures—the tropical tortoise and the spider monkey. These animals are primarily fruit eaters, and they regularly disperse the seeds of dense hardwood trees in tropical regions. In turn, those trees, when fully grown, are major absorbers of carbon dioxide from the atmosphere. They not only generate precious supplies of oxygen but also help keep the greenhouse effect from running amok by lowering levels of carbon dioxide. As science writer Damian Carrington sums it up,

> When scientists explore each ecosystem, they find count-less such interactions, all honed by millions of years of evolu-tion. If undamaged, this produces a finely balanced, healthy system which contributes to a healthy sustainable planet.

> The sheer richness of biodiversity also has human ben-efits. Many new medicines are harvested from nature, for instance, such as a fungus that grows on the fur of sloths and can fight cancer.[35]

Climate-Influenced Genetic Changes

Given that maintaining as much natural biodiversity as possible is essential to human civilization, losses of biodiversity due to climate change and other factors have recently become major subjects of scientific scrutiny. Detailed scientific snapshots, so to speak, of diverse plant and animal species—including the 2018–2019 UN and WWF studies—show that huge numbers of spe-cies are struggling. Those struggles are taking place on both the micro and macro levels.

"Many new medicines are harvested from nature, for instance, such as a fungus that grows on the fur of sloths and can fight cancer."[35]

—Science writer Damian Carrington

What Is Biodiversity?

Biodiversity "is the variety of life on Earth, in all its forms and all its interactions," explains science writer Damian Carrington. He describes biodiversity as the planet's most complex and vital feature, adding that

> the huge global biodiversity losses now becoming apparent represent a crisis equaling, or quite possibly surpassing, climate change. More formally, biodiversity is comprised of several levels, starting with genes, then individual species, then communities of creatures, and finally entire ecosystems, such as forests or coral reefs, where life interplays with the physical environment. These myriad [many] interactions have made Earth habitable for billions of years. A more philosophical way of viewing biodiversity is this: it represents the knowledge learned by evolving species over millions of years about how to survive through the vastly varying environmental conditions Earth has experienced. For many people living in towns and cities, wildlife is often something you watch on television. But the reality is that the air you breathe, the water you drink and the food you eat all ultimately rely on biodiversity.

Damian Carrington, "What Is Biodiversity and Why Does It Matter to Us?," *Guardian*, March 12, 2018. www.theguardian.com.

On the micro, or microscopic, level, many species are reacting to the warming climate and weather extremes by changing on a genetic level. In one of many recorded examples, warmer atmospheric temperatures have been slowly but steadily lengthening the spring and summer seasons in the Appalachian Mountains. In response, the region's woodland salamanders are growing physically smaller with each succeeding generation. Similarly, the long-billed red knot bird, which breeds in the Arctic, is having progressively smaller young; in one of many examples of evolution in action, the bills of the offspring are getting shorter. The longer growing seasons in the Americas are also producing more food for some species. These include squirrel-like marmots and weasel-like martens, both of which have been growing bigger.

Meanwhile, climatic changes in recent decades have caused evolutionary changes in a number of other creatures. For example, alpine chipmunks in Yellowstone National Park in Wyoming have undergone noticeable changes in the shape of their skulls. Also, the habitat of one of their relatives—the northern flying squirrel—has been growing warmer. As a result, another relative—the southern flying squirrel—has expanded northward and is mating with its northern cousin. At the same time, the changing genes of pink salmon are causing them to migrate earlier than ever before. Even the lowly water flea is experiencing measurable genetic changes in response to higher water temperatures.

The occurrence of such genetic alterations does not necessarily mean that these species are successfully adapting to the warm-

Climate change has physically affected various bird species, including the long-billed red knot, seen here. Their bills are getting smaller, and many have been producing progressively smaller chicks.

ing global climate. In fact, says University of Florida scientist Bret Scheffers, "in many instances genetic diversity is being lost due to climate change." He cautions that "it is important not to confuse species responses and adaptation as an indicator that everything will be okay."[36] Rather, he says, many of these spontaneous attempts to adapt have failed or will eventually fail, and no meaningful species survival will occur. As a result, he adds, 47 percent of land mammals and 23 percent of birds have already suffered negative impacts from climate change. "Given what we are seeing now," says John Wiens, a professor at the University of Arizona, "just imagine what will happen to all these species when temperatures increase by [a factor of] four or five times."[37]

"In many instances genetic diversity is being lost due to climate change."[36]

—University of Florida scientist Bret Scheffers

Death in the Arctic and Antarctic

Disruptive and destructive changes are also happening to many species on the larger, more visible macro level. Like species on the micro level, they are witnessing transformations of their natural habitats that are too big and rapid for them to cope with constructively. Particularly troubled are animals that traditionally dwell in cold climates and are strongly feeling the effects of the warming atmosphere and oceans. The most familiar example of this is the Arctic polar bear. According to environmental journalist Stephen Leahy,

> Best estimates say there are 20,000 to 30,000 polar bears in 19 different groups or populations scattered across the top of the U.S., Canada, Greenland, Norway, and Russia. Four of these populations are considered to be declining. Bears in the Beaufort Sea region are among the best studied and their numbers have fallen 40 percent in the last ten years.[38]

This ongoing decline in the polar bear population has been confirmed to be principally caused by starvation, which is directly linked to climate change. Although the bears are strong swimmers, by instinct their main hunting routine is to search out their primary prey—seals—on floating Arctic ice sheets. The number of those sheets—and their size—has been swiftly decreasing in recent decades. This has forced the huge creatures to walk and swim increasingly farther distances to find the ice they require for hunting. "The farther the bears have to travel to get on the ice to hunt," Leahy writes, "the more weight they lose. Eventually they

Threats to Coral Reefs

Coral reefs feature the largest biodiversity of any global ecosystem. Each healthy, intact reef supports hundreds or even thousands of marine species, and more than 500 million people around the world, primarily in poor countries, depend on those species for food. Coral reefs are also among the most threatened ecosystems on the planet, mainly because of warming ocean waters resulting from climate change. According to the International Union for Conservation of Nature, a group of more than ten thousand scientists and other environmental experts,

> When conditions such as the temperature change, corals expel the symbiotic algae [interdependent microbes] living in their tissues, responsible for their color. A spike of 1–2°C in ocean temperatures sustained over several weeks can lead to bleaching, turning corals white. If corals are bleached for prolonged periods, they eventually die. Coral bleaching events often lead to the death of large amounts of corals. . . . [In recent years] iconic reefs such as the Great Barrier Reef in Australia and the Northwestern Hawaiian Islands in the United States have all experienced their worst bleaching on record with devastating effects. The bleaching of the Great Barrier Reef in 2016 and 2017, for instance, killed around 50% of its corals. Corals cannot survive the frequency of current bleaching events from global temperature rise. If temperatures continue to rise, bleaching events will increase in intensity and frequency.

International Union for Conservation of Nature, "Coral Reefs and Climate Change," November 2017. www.iucn.org.

start losing muscle, hurting their chances of hunting success, which can lead to a downward spiral."[39] Making matters worse, zoologists point out that female polar bears stop having babies when their weight drops below about 400 pounds (181 kg).

The noble-looking white Arctic bears are not the only ice-dependent animals that are nearing the brink of extinction because of climate change. Walruses are struggling as well, in large part because they instinctively feed and nurse their young on the ice sheets. A similar scenario has been playing out on the far

In December 2017, a starving polar bear desperately searches for food. Climate change has significantly reduced hunting opportunities for the species, which is threatened with extinction.

side of the globe, in Antarctica. Emperor penguins—the largest of all penguin species—breed and raise their young on floating ice sheets. When the warming climate combined forces with a large ocean storm in 2016, the world's second-largest emperor penguin colony suddenly collapsed. Upwards of ten thousand chicks perished, and experts estimate that many thousands of eggs were destroyed. The colony never rebounded.

Disturbing Insect Losses

Another macro example of animal species either recently extinct or nearing the verge of complete elimination involves creatures that have traditionally been among the most numerous on the planet—insects. According to a study in the journal *Science*, the numbers in each of hundreds of common insect species, including several kinds of beetles, shrank by up to 45 percent between about 1980 and 2014. The situation is even worse with flying insects, the researchers pointed out, which decreased in number as much as 76 percent in some parts of the world during the same period.

Biologist Bradford Lister calls this ominous trend "disturbing." Referring to the high number of insect species that are growing less abundant, he adds, "Everything is dropping."[40] In addition to beetles, he says, common insects like bees, grasshoppers, moths, and butterflies display similar losses. The same is true of spiders and some other arachnids.

Lister and other scientists blame climate change for most of these losses. Over the past forty years, they say, the average temperatures in rain forests worldwide have increased by four degrees Fahrenheit. The tiny insects and arachnids cannot regulate their internal temperature well enough to keep pace with what is to them extremely rapid and damaging change. As a result, they are dying in large numbers.

One very real danger of this trend is that some of those creatures are pollinators. Around 40 percent of all flowering plants—

some 300,000 plant species in all, including many food crops—must be pollinated by bees and other insects. Those insect pollinators are rapidly disappearing. As a result, Lister warns, some plant species, particularly in the world's tropical rain forests, have already gone extinct, and many more will die out in each succeeding year. "If the tropical forests go," he states, "it will be yet another catastrophic failure of the whole earth system. That will feed back on human beings in an almost unimaginable way."[41]

> "If the tropical forests go, it will be yet another catastrophic failure of the whole earth system."[41]
>
> —Biologist Bradford Lister

Thus, looking at human-generated damage to other species in general, the outlook for later in this century appears grim. Yet serious threats to animals and plants are no longer merely vague predictions of what might happen in the distant future. Nature is under attack now, and what threatens nature also threatens the human race. "This is far more than just being about losing the wonders of nature, desperately sad though that is," says Mike Barrett, the executive director of science at the WWF. "This is actually now jeopardizing the future of people. Nature is not just 'nice to have.' It is our life-support system."[42]

CHAPTER 5

Fighting and Adapting to Climate Change

Considering that climate change is already negatively affecting local communities, cities, and entire nations around the world, it is not surprising that various efforts are already under way to deal with it. These efforts are of three basic kinds. The first, which is mostly political and diplomatic in nature, takes the form of international agreements, whereby countries agree to address the overall problem of climate change.

The second major ongoing approach to dealing with climate change is to physically reduce greenhouse gas emissions in order to slow the ongoing warming of the planet's atmosphere. That process is already under way in many countries. It consists mainly of switching from older, dirtier energy-producing methods, like burning coal, to clean ones, such as solar and wind power.

Finally, the third approach to dealing with climate change is to devise ways to adapt to the changing conditions. Those governments and communities that have embarked on this path accept that the world's climate has already changed and will continue to do so for the foreseeable future. They believe that they will better prosper by learning to adapt to and live with that change even while trying to stop any further atmospheric warming.

International Agreements

Diplomatic efforts to deal with climate change on an international scale date back to the 1990s. But the largest and most far-reaching climate-change treaty—the Paris Agreement—was signed by 195 nations, including the United States, in 2016. It stipulated that each country had to make a plan to fight climate change and regularly report on its progress in instituting that plan. In 2017, however, a new US president, Donald Trump, announced that the United States would withdraw from the Paris Agreement in 2020 (the soonest the withdrawal could occur under the terms of the treaty). He claimed that the agreement treats the United States unfairly, requiring more of it than of other major polluters such as China and India. This view has been disputed. Nevertheless, in 2019 the United States was still on track to withdraw from the Paris Agreement.

Not content to rely on the federal government for a response to climate change, many US states have chosen to act on their own. For example, nine New England and mid-Atlantic states—Vermont, New Hampshire, Maine, Connecticut, New York, Massachusetts, New Jersey, Delaware, and Maryland—have formed a pact called the Regional Greenhouse Gas Initiative (RGGI). The group's goal is to reduce greenhouse gas emissions by promoting and using cleaner energy-producing methods, including solar and wind power. Every three years the members will set a new goal to reduce their emissions by a certain percentage, often as high as 10 percent.

Moving Toward Cleaner Energy

In an effort to slow the advance of climate change, many nations are, like the states in the RGGI, in the process of reducing their reliance on fossil fuels and switching to cleaner energy sources. These sources are known as renewable energy. They include hydroelectric power, created by moving water that spins turbines; power from wind-driven turbines; solar, or sun-generated, power of various kinds; and geothermal power, which draws energy from heat rising up from deep inside the planet. These methods, along with other green technologies, produce electricity with few or no harmful emissions or pollutants. Potentially, the most plentiful renewable source of power is solar energy. This is because

Wind farms like this one are becoming increasingly common in the United States. By using more clean, renewable energy sources like wind power, humanity can reduce its production of greenhouse gases.

of the enormous amount of sunlight that strikes our planet every day. For instance, in only seventy-one minutes, Earth receives enough solar radiation to power all of human civilization for an entire year. Science has not yet achieved the ability to actually capture the bulk of that sunlight. As a result, hydroelectric power from turbines operating at large dams presently contributes more usable energy than solar and other renewables.

However, that situation is rapidly changing. The International Renewable Energy Agency (IRENA), established by the UN in 1981, reported in 2019 that renewables were providing up to one-third of the electrical power in many cities and towns around the globe. That was an enormous advance considering that less than 5 percent of electrical power came from renewables before 2009. Moreover, IRENA found that fully two-thirds of the electrical capacity added to human civilization in 2018 was from renewables. Of that total, 84 percent came from wind and solar sources alone.

Has Climate Change Made Poor Nations Poorer?

According to the results of a Stanford University study released in 2019, in recent years climate change has widened the gap between rich and poor countries. Moreover, that has made both fighting and adapting to climate change more difficult for smaller, poorer nations. One of the study's authors, Stanford professor Marshall Burke, carefully analyzed data about the relationship between temperature changes and economic growth in 165 countries between 1961 and 2010. He also used a computer to calculate alternate versions of what those nations' annual growth rates would have been if climate change had not been a factor.

The results of Burke's study were revealing. They showed that in rich countries like the United States, Canada, and the United Kingdom, economic growth increased in the target period. These nations are in cooler latitudes, Burke points out, and slight increases in global temperatures actually benefited their growing seasons. In contrast, in poorer nations in Africa and southern Asia, where it was already very warm year-round, economic growth slowed down. This is because the extra warmth made it too hot to produce food and other resources in needed quantities. Thus, Burke concludes that climate change has made nations that were poor to begin with even more impoverished.

Quoted in Pablo Uchoa, "How Global Warming Has Made the Rich Richer," BBC World Service, May 6, 2019. www.bbc.com.

In fact, energy experts now conclude that renewables, led by wind, solar, and hydroelectric, represent the future of electrical energy production. IRENA director-general Adnan Z. Amin remarked in 2019, "The strong growth [of renewables] in 2018 continues the remarkable trend of the last five years, which reflects an ongoing shift towards renewable power as the driver of global energy transformation."[43]

The Union of Concerned Scientists (UCS) notes that two vital goals can be accomplished by steadily replacing fossil fuels with renewable sources. First, it can provide most or all the energy needed to power civilization. Also, because renewables do not pollute and do not emit greenhouse gases, they can slow and perhaps even stop the relentless onrush of climate change. In the United States alone, the UCS states,

> strong winds, sunny skies, plant residues, heat from the earth, and fast-moving water can each provide a vast and constantly replenished energy resource supply. . . . [Furthermore,] increasing the supply of renewable energy would allow us to replace carbon-intensive energy sources and significantly reduce US global warming emissions.[44]

Copenhagen: The Model Green City

Efforts to slow climate change go beyond shifting to renewable energy sources. Leading the way in this regard is Denmark's capital city of Copenhagen (population 624,000). Beginning in the early 2000s, city officials introduced rules and infrastructure changes designed to significantly reduce the city's carbon footprint, or the amount of carbon dioxide it produces. First, they placed serious limitations on greenhouse gas emissions from local factories. They also moved to eliminate most cars and other gas-burning vehicles by switching to greener, more energy-efficient forms of transportation. This included building a new subway system with at least one station in every neighborhood and expanding the length and width of bicycle paths to encourage more bicycling. In addition, they installed new high-tech incinerators that heat buildings while efficiently burning garbage. Finally, to boost energy production while maintaining zero emissions, the city erected numerous large wind turbines.

"Strong winds, sunny skies, plant residues, heat from the earth, and fast-moving water can each provide a vast and constantly replenished energy resource supply."[44]

—The Union of Concerned Scientists

Overall, Copenhagen's attempt to go green has been a swift and resounding success. Its greenhouse gas emissions shrank significantly between 2005 and 2019. City officials predict emissions will reach zero in 2025. Early in 2019, Copenhagen's mayor, Frank Jensen, proudly declared that people *"can change the way we behave, the way we are living, and go more green."*[45]

Capturing Carbon from the Air

Few cities or countries have gone as far as Copenhagen in altering business, industry, and lifestyle to reduce greenhouse gases. Instead, some hope to slow the advance of climate change by scrubbing the atmosphere of carbon dioxide. One of the more promising technologies developed for this purpose is known as a carbon-capture machine. These machines quite literally remove carbon dioxide from the air and concentrate it in units that can be sold for use in various industries. For instance, various forms of carbon dioxide are used in refrigeration and cooling and in the manufacture of fire extinguishers and casting molds.

Global Thermostat, located in Huntsville, Alabama, and Climeworks, based in Switzerland, are only two of several small new companies that are dedicated to carbon capture. A few larger corporations, including some major oil companies, are experimenting with the process as well. The owners of these companies realize that a lot of money can potentially be made capturing carbon from the air. "Our business plan is to show that cleaning the atmosphere is a profitable activity,"[46] says Global Thermostat cofounder Graciela Chichilnisky. She is convinced that the carbon-capture industry will eventually do trillions of dollars of business per year.

Global Thermostat and the other similar companies use large vacuum pumps to capture carbon dioxide. These pumps suck air into boxes that are the size of large shipping containers. Inside each box are ceramic tubes arranged in clusters that resemble honeycombs. The tubes contain chemicals that act like filters or sponges; they absorb carbon dioxide. Once saturated, the tubes are heated; that process causes the release of carbon dioxide into a storage tank.

As of 2019, carbon-capture efforts such as this were still occurring on a very small scale. The company executives involved freely admit that tens of thousands of such machines would need to operate all day, every day on a worldwide basis to make even a small dent in reducing global carbon dioxide levels. They are confident, however, that the technology will improve and expand over time. The hope is that it will be a useful supplement to the larger effort to reduce greenhouse gas emissions.

This innovative plant run by Climeworks in Zurich, Switzerland, removes carbon dioxide from the atmosphere and then sells it to farmers, scientists, and others who require that substance for their work.

Learning to Adapt to Climate Change

Reducing greenhouse gases remains a priority for many government and business entities worldwide, but some are embarking on a different path. The reality of a warming planet has led some groups to focus on adaptation. This is the idea that humanity must learn how to live on a changed planet. This means learning to produce crops in different growing seasons; developing crops that are more tolerant of drought; getting used to altered weather patterns; changing building codes that allow for more extreme weather events; raising the height of existing levees and dykes to prevent flooding; and using forestry practices that are less vulnerable to large-scale fires. A growing number of experts say that doing such things will help humanity adjust to the conditions brought about by climate change and thereby prevent mass suffering.

One of the leading efforts to accomplish this goal began in 2017. Called the Columbia World Projects Program, it is sponsored by Columbia University's International Research Institute for Climate and Society (IRI). Its chief project is ACToday, short for "Adapting Agriculture to Climate Today, for Tomorrow." Its main goal is to fight hunger in six nations that are especially dependent on agriculture and already feeling the effects of climate change. The countries are Bangladesh, Colombia, Ethiopia, Guatemala, Senegal, and Vietnam. The program works primarily through increasing knowledge in those nations about climate, weather, and how each is presently affecting their food production.

In Vietnam, for example, food production had suffered during prior generations because of the ravages of war and famine. Over time, local farmers recovered from those setbacks but then came up against climate change. Rising temperatures shortened growing seasons in the north. Meanwhile, the nation's most productive region—the Mekong Delta—began to be affected by sea-level rise and the intrusion of saltwater into the soil, making it increasingly difficult to grow some staple crops. Local farmers were initially unable to cope with these changing conditions, in

Jamaica Adapts to Climate Change

One of the world's most successful efforts to adapt to climate change so far has occurred in the Caribbean island nation of Jamaica. From the late twentieth century on, Jamaica has been repeatedly battered by large storms that have been strengthened by climate change. Flooding resulting from those storms has killed hundreds of islanders and has caused hundreds of millions of dollars in damage. Seeing that devastation, the Jamaican government decided that the best approach was to accept the reality of bigger storms and adapt to them. In 2013 it launched the Climate Change and Inland Flooding in Jamaica: Risk and Adaptation Measures for Vulnerable Communities plan. The project created detailed maps that use the latest computerized storm and flood predictions to pinpoint where the worst flooding will happen as climate change steadily worsens. The idea is to use these improved flood models, along with other information, to educate farmers and other residents. They can then work in partnership with the government to reduce the impact of future storms and floods by building levees, dams, runoff systems, and other flood-prevention projects. According to the project's website, the data compiled on the updated maps has become a vital

> decision-making tool that assists policy-makers in creating or revising effective flood mitigation measures, evacuation strategies, and national disaster risk management plans. Additionally, it helps determine the adaptation measures that can be adopted by communities to respond to increasing flood risk, and protect those most vulnerable.

Climate & Development Knowledge Network, "Project: Climate Change and Inland Flooding in Jamaica: Risk and Adaptation Measures for Vulnerable Communities." https://cdkn.org.

part because they lacked the most accurate climate information and expertise in how to adjust to such radical changes. The IRI program provides information and training to help those farmers adjust their growing schedules and methods. The institute also assists government agencies with low-interest loan programs for farmers.

Similar programs and initiatives based on adapting to climate change can be seen in other countries. Only a few include Cuba

Rising sea levels caused by climate change have allowed saltwater to leak into the soil in Vietnam's principal farming region, the Mekong Delta. A bold Columbia University project is teaching local farmers to cope.

and the island countries of Palau and Kiribati in the Pacific Ocean. These nations are educating their citizens about the steadily warming world. They are also instituting programs designed to help their most vulnerable populations adapt to changing conditions. In Cuba, for instance, the government has stopped all new construction in coastal areas that are threatened by flooding from sea-level rise. According to journalists Yisell R. Milán and Danae G. Del Toro, other actions taken by the Cuban government include "reducing cultivated areas along the coastline and in areas affected by saltwater intrusion, diversifying crops, improving soils, and introducing and developing varieties resistant to higher temperatures."[47]

"We [at the World Bank] are pushing ourselves to do more and to go faster on climate and we call on the global community to do the same."[48]

—Jim Yong Kim, president of the World Bank Group

Looking for a Bigger, Faster Response

Even as some of the world's governments begin efforts to adapt to the effects of climate change, scientists and international leaders recognize that more must be done. In December 2018 Jim Yong Kim, the president of the World Bank Group, announced new investments of about $200 billion to support more ambitious actions on climate change. The threat to the world's poorest people and to the rest of the world is dire. That threat, he warned, requires a much bigger and much faster response: "We [at the World Bank] are pushing ourselves to do more and to go faster on climate and we call on the global community to do the same. This is about putting countries and communities in charge of building a safer, more climate-resilient future."[48]

SOURCE NOTES

Introduction: Climate Change Is Already Happening

1. Quoted in GlobalChange.gov, "Climate Change." www.global change.gov.
2. Quoted in Alejandro de la Garza, "President Trump Renews Climate Change Denial Days After Defense Department Releases Daunting Report on Its Effects," *Time,* January 20, 2019. https://time.com.
3. NASA, "What Is the Greenhouse Effect?," June 2019. https://climatekids.nasa.gov.
4. National Oceanic and Atmospheric Association (NOAA), "2018 Was 4th Hottest Year on Record for the Globe," February 2019. www.noaa.gov.
5. Quoted in World Wildlife Fund, "10 Myths About Climate Change." www.wwf.org.uk.

Chapter 1: An Onslaught of Extreme Weather Events

6. Quoted in Marie D. Aronsohn, "What Do Cold Snaps Have to Do with Climate Change?," January 2018. https://phys.org.
7. Rebecca Lindsey, "Exceptional Drought in Parts of Seven States in U.S. Southwest," NOAA, April 2018. www.climate.gov.
8. Quoted in Zoeann Murphy and Chris Mooney, "Gone in a Generation: Across America Climate Change Is Already Disrupting Lives," *Washington Post,* January 2019. www.washingtonpost.com.
9. Union of Concerned Scientists, "Hurricanes and Climate Change." www.ucsusa.org.
10. Quoted in Senate Democrats, "What Will It Take for Senate Republicans to Recognize Climate Change Is Real and Finally Do Something About It?," March 2019. www.democrats.senate.gov.

11. Quoted in Senate Democrats, "What Will It Take for Senate Republicans to Recognize Climate Change Is Real and Finally Do Something About It?"
12. American Meteorological Society, "Heatwaves, Droughts, and Floods Among Recent Weather Extremes Linked to Climate Change," December 2018. www.ametsoc.org.
13. Quoted in Brandon Miller, "Climate Change Is Not Only Influencing Extreme Weather Events, It's Causing Them," CNN, December 10, 2018. www.cnn.com.

Chapter 2: The Ongoing Threat of Sea-Level Rise
14. Quoted in Daniel Glick, "The Big Thaw: As the Climate Warms, How Much, and How Quickly, Will Earth's Glaciers Melt?," *National Geographic.* www.nationalgeographic.com.
15. Quoted in European Space Agency, "Glaciers Lose Nine Trillion Tons of Ice in Half a Century," April 8, 2019. ww.esa.int.
16. National Snow and Ice Data Center (NSIDC), "Rapid Ice Loss in Early April Leads to New Record Low," May 2, 2019. https://nsidc.org.
17. NSIDC, "Rapid Ice Loss in Early April Leads to New Record Low."
18. Quoted in Laura Naranjo, "After the Larsen B," May 8, 2019. https://earthdata.nasa.gov.
19. Naranjo, "After the Larsen B."
20. William Sweet and John Marra, "Understanding Climate: Billy Sweet and John Marra Explain Nuisance Floods," NOAA, September 8, 2015. www.climate.gov.
21. Robin McKie, "Miami, the Great World City, Is Drowning While the Powers That Be Look Away," *Guardian,* July 22, 2014. www.theguardian.com.
22. Mary Mazzoni, "3p Weekend: 5 Cities Already Feeling the Effects of Climate Change," Triple Pundit, July 18, 2014. www.triplepundit.com.

Chapter 3: Climate Change and Global Food Supply
23. Center for Climate and Life, "Food," Columbia University. http://climateandlife.columbia.edu.

24 Acciona, "Impacts of Climate Change on Wine." www.active sustainability.com.

25. Quoted in Renee Cho, "How Climate Change Will Alter Our Food," *State of the Planet* (blog), Earth Institute, Columbia University, July 25, 2018. https://blogs.ei.columbia.edu.

26. Alycia Drwencke, Cassandra Tucker, and Theresa Pistochini, "Scientists Explain How to Reduce Heat Stress in Cows Before It's Too Late," Conversation, October 2, 2018. http://the conversation.com.

27. Reuters, "Ocean Shock: The Planet's Hidden Climate Change," October 20, 2018. www.reuters.com.

28. Quoted in Kendra Pierre-Louis, "The World Is Losing Fish to Eat as Oceans Warm, Study Finds," *New York Times,* February 28, 2019. www.nytimes.com.

29. Quoted in Rob Hotakainen, "Warming Waters Spark Marine Migration, Fish Wars," *E&E News,* May 28, 2019. www.eenews.net.

30. Quoted in Hotakainen, "Warming Waters Spark Marine Migration, Fish Wars."

31. Pierre-Louis, "The World Is Losing Fish to Eat as Oceans Warm, Study Finds."

Chapter 4: Ongoing Losses of Species and Biodiversity

32. Quoted in Brooks Hays, "U.N.: 1M Species Threatened as Global Extinction Rates Speed Up," UPI, May 6, 2019. www.upi.com.

33. Quoted in Hays, "U.N."

34. Quoted in Damian Carrington, "Humanity Has Wiped Out 60% of Animal Populations Since 1970, Report Finds," *Guardian,* October 29, 2018. www.theguardian.com.

35. Damian Carrington, "What Is Biodiversity and Why Does It Matter to Us?," *Guardian,* March 12, 2018. www.theguardian.com.

36. Quoted in Jeremy Hance, "Climate Change Impacting 'Most' Species on Earth, Even Down to Their Genomes," *Guardian,* April 5, 2017. www.theguardian.com.

37. Quoted in Hance, "Climate Change Impacting 'Most' Species on Earth, Even Down to Their Genomes."

38. Stephen Leahy, "Polar Bears Really Are Starving Because of Global Warming, Study Shows," *National Geograhic,* February 1, 2018. https://news.nationalgeographic.com.

39. Leahy, "Polar Bears Really Are Starving Because of Global Warming, Study Shows."

40. Quoted in Ben Guarino, "'Hyperalarming' Study Shows Massive Insect Loss," *Washington Post,* October 15, 2018. www.washingtonpost.com.

41. Quoted in Guarino, "'Hyperalarming' Study Shows Massive Insect Loss."

42. Quoted in Carrington, "Humanity Has Wiped Out 60% of Animal Populations Since 1970, Report Finds."

Chapter 5: Fighting and Adapting to Climate Change

43. Quoted in John Parnell, "One-Third of World's Power Plant Capacity Is Now Renewable," *Forbes,* April 3, 2019. www.forbes.com.

44. Union of Concerned Scientists, "Benefits of Renewable Energy Use," December 20, 2017. www.ucsusa.org.

45. Quoted in Somini Sengupta, "Copenhagen Wants to Show How Cities Can Fight Climate Change," *New York Times,* March 25, 2019. www.nytimes.com.

46. Quoted in Steven Mufson, "A Climate Change Solution Slowly Gains Ground," *Washington Post,* April 19, 2019. www.washingtonpost.com.

47. Yisell R. Milán and Danae G. Del Toro, "Project Life: Cuba's Action Plan Prepares for Climate Change," *Climate & Capitalism,* April 13, 2018. https://climateandcapitalism.com.

48. Quoted in World Bank, "World Bank Group Announces $200 Billion over Five Years for Climate Action," December 2018. www.worldbank.org.

ORGANIZATIONS TO CONTACT

Center for Climate and Energy Solutions (C2ES) —
www.c2es.org

C2ES, formerly called the Pew Center on Global Climate Change, promotes reducing carbon dioxide emissions and adopting cleaner energy solutions. The website features links to information on how both individuals and groups can support the C2ES and thereby help fight climate change.

GlobalChange.gov — www.globalchange.gov

This website includes the colorful, graphics-filled article "Climate Change," which presents the main findings of climate scientists on the present climate crisis. The website contains many links to related topics.

Intergovernmental Panel on Climate Change (IPCC) —
www.ipcc.ch

The IPCC is the leading international organization presently studying and fighting climate change. The website provides up-to-date reports on the activities of several IPCC working groups, and also tells how students and other everyday people can get involved in efforts to stop climate change.

National Aeronautics and Space Administration (NASA) —
https://climate.nasa.gov

This section of the NASA website, "Global Climate Change: Vital Signs of the Planet," provides excellent facts, explanations, articles, graphics, and more on the topic of climate change.

National Center for Atmospheric Research (NCAR) —
https://ncar.ucar.edu

NCAR's website has a number of links to articles about present efforts to fight climate change. Included are numerous dramatic photos of damage done by hurricanes and fires made worse by climate change, along with information on how students can intern with NCAR.

National Oceanic and Atmospheric Administration (NOAA) —
www.noaa.org

NOAA's main website provides a simple definition for climate change, along with links to helpful articles on the subject. There are also links to climate predictions by scientists and information from the National Weather Service.

Natural Resources Defense Council (NRDC) — www.nrdc.org

The NRDC's mission is to protect humanity's clean air and water and natural wildlife. The group's website contains several links to explanations of how the residents of individual towns and neighborhoods can get involved in the effort to stop the ravages of climate change.

Science News for Students —
www.sciencenewsforstudents.org

This award-winning online publication provides topical science news on a wide array of science topics, including many articles about different aspects of climate change.

World Meteorological Organization (WMO) —
https://public.wmo.int

The WMO's website has many links to articles relating to global weather patterns and how they affect human civilization. Students will find links to helpful publications about climate change, and a "WMO for Youth" section provides entertaining activities related to fighting climate change.

Books

Anthony McMichael, *Climate Change and the Health of Nations.* New York: Oxford University Press, 2019.

New York Times Editorial Staff, *Climate Change*. New York: New York Times Educational and Rosen, 2019.

New York Times Editorial Staff, *Climate Refugees: How Climate Change Is Displacing Millions*. New York: New York Times Educational and Rosen, 2019.

Joseph Romm, *Climate Change: What Everyone Needs to Know.* New York: Oxford University Press, 2018.

Internet Sources

Alejandra Borunda, "2018 Was the U.S.'s Third-Wettest Year on Record—Here's Why," *National Geographic,* February 7, 2019. www.nationalgeographic.com.

Daniel Glick, "The Big Thaw: As the Climate Warms, How Much, and How Quickly, Will Earth's Glaciers Melt?," *National Geographic.* www.nationalgeographic.com.

International Research Group for Science and Society, "Adapting Agriculture to Climate Today, for Tomorrow." https://iri.columbia.edu.

Matt McGrath, "Final Call to Save the World from 'Climate Catastrophe,'" BBC News, October 8, 2018. www.bbc.com.

Christina Nunez, "Ocean Species Are Disappearing Faster than Those on Land," *National Geographic,* April 24, 2019. www.nationalgeographic.com.

Kendra Pierre-Louis, "The World Is Losing Fish to Eat as Oceans Warm, Study Finds," *New York Times,* February 28, 2019. www.nytimes.com.

Reuters, "Ocean Shock: The Climate Crisis Beneath the Waves." www.reuters.com.

Nassos Stylianou et al., "Climate Change: Where We are in Seven Charts and What You Can Do to Help," BBC News, April 18, 2019. www.bbc.com.

Reports

American Meteorological Society, "Explaining Extreme Events from a Climate Perspective," 2018. www.ametsoc.org.

IPCC, *Special Report: Global Warming of 1.5 °C*, 2018. www.ip cc.ch.

United Nations Environment Programme, "Global Environment Outlook: Healthy Planet, Healthy People," Cambridge University, 2019. https://content.yudu.com/web/2y3n2/0A2y3n3/GEO6/html /index.html?origin=reader.

US Global Change Research Program, *Fourth National Climate Assessment,* 2018. https://nca2018.globalchange.gov.

World Health Organization, *COP24 Special Report: Health & Climate Change*, 2018. www.who.int.

INDEX

PICTURE CREDITS

ABOUT THE AUTHOR

In addition to his numerous acclaimed volumes on ancient civilizations, historian Don Nardo has published several studies of scientific discoveries and phenomena, including *Sustainable Energy*, *Polar Explorations*, *Volcanoes*, *The Scientific Revolution*, and *How Vaccines Changed the World*, as well as award-winning books on astronomy and space exploration. Mr. Nardo also composes and arranges orchestral music. He lives with his wife, Christine, in Massachusetts.